Jeff Gordon

by Rosemary Wallner

Reading Consultant:
Dr. Robert Miller
Professor of Special Education
Minnesota State University

C A P S T O N E   B O O K S

an imprint of Capstone Press
Mankato, Minnesota

Capstone Books are published by Capstone Press
151 Good Counsel Drive, P.O. Box 669, Mankato, Minnesota 56002
http://www.capstone-press.com

Library of Congress Cataloging-in-Publication Data
Wallner, Rosemary, 1964–
    Jeff Gordon/by Rosemary Wallner.
    p. cm.—(Sports heroes)
    Includes bibliographical references (p. 44) and index.
    Summary: Discusses the racing career, life, and accomplishments of the youngest
driver to win the Winston Cup title.
    ISBN 0-7368-0577-X
    1. Gordon, Jeff, 1971—Juvenile literature. 2. Automobile racing drivers—United
States—Biography—Juvenile literature. [1. Gordon, Jeff, 1971– 2. Automobile racing
drivers.] I. Title. II. Sports heroes (Mankato, Minn.).
GV1032.G67 W25 2001
796.72'092—dc21
[B]   00-024476

Editorial Credits
Matt Doeden, editor; Timothy Halldin, cover designer and illustrator; Heidi Schoof and
    Kimberly Danger, photo researchers

Photo Credits
Active Images, Inc./Greg Crisp, 18, 20, 26, 28, 32, 36, 46
AP World Wide Photos, cover; Steve Helber, 7; John Bazemore, 40
Isaac Hernandez/Mercury Press, 31
Janine Pestel, 10, 23
Joseph Pestel, 9, 24, 43
SportsChrome-USA/Greg Crisp, 4, 39; Rob Tringali Jr., 13, 14;
    Brian Spurlock, 17; Louis Raymon, 34

1 2 3 4 5 6 06 05 04 03 02 01

Table of Contents

CHAPTER 1

An Important Race

On October 3, 1999, Jeff Gordon was on the 485th lap of the Auto Care 500 in Martinsville, Virginia. He was among the race's leaders with 15 laps to go. But the tires on his car were worn from driving. Jeff watched many of the race's other leaders make pit stops for new tires. He knew that he would lose his place among the leaders if he stopped. He could win the race if his tires would last 15 more laps.

This race was especially important to Jeff and his racing team. It was his first

Jeff Gordon is one of NASCAR's top drivers.

race without his long-time crew chief, Ray Evernham. Evernham had quit the team the week before the race to take charge of a different team. A new crew chief named Brian Whitesell had taken Evernham's place. Jeff wanted to prove that he could win with Whitesell as his crew chief.

Earlier in the race, Jeff had been as far behind as 16th place. But he and Whitesell still believed they could win. They decided together that Jeff should not make a pit stop for new tires late in the race. This decision was dangerous. Worn tires can make a car difficult to control. Jeff could not drive as fast as he normally could.

Driver Dale Earnhardt came up close behind Jeff's car on the final lap of the race. Earnhardt's car had fresh tires and better speed than Jeff's car. But Jeff held onto the lead and crossed the finish line. After the race, he said that he had never wanted to win so badly.

Jeff won the Auto Care 500 on October 3, 1999.

About Jeff Gordon

Jeff Gordon is a stock car driver. He drives a Chevrolet Monte Carlo in NASCAR's Winston Cup Series. His car's number is 24. Jeff started racing in NASCAR's top division at the end of the 1992 racing season. By 1999, he had won three championships. In 1998, he tied a NASCAR record for the most wins in one season. He won 13 races that season.

Jeff also is successful off the race track. His fan club includes more than 15,000 members. He helps run an Internet site that has thousands of visitors every week. Jeff even has NASCAR video games named after him.

Jeff Gordon

Winston Cup Finishes

Year	Starts	Wins	Top 5	Top 10	Winnings
1992	1	0	0	0	$6,285
1993	30	0	7	11	$765,168
1994	31	2	7	14	$1,779,523
1995	31	7	10	16	$4,347,343
1996	31	10	21	24	$3,428,485
1997	32	10	22	23	$6,375,658
1998	33	13	26	28	$5,158,392
1999	34	7	18	21	$5,121,361
Total	223	49	111	137	$26,982,215

CHAPTER 2

The Early Years

Jeff Gordon was born August 4, 1971, in Vallejo, California. His mother, Carol, was an office manager. Jeff has an older sister named Kim. Carol married John Bickford when Jeff was 4 years old. John was an auto parts manufacturer. He also was a racing fan. John became Jeff's stepfather.

An Early Interest in Racing

Jeff became interested in racing at age 4. He began to ride a bicycle that year. He often rode very fast down a hill near his home. Jeff also took part in his first official races. He rode in

Jeff has enjoyed racing all of his life.

bicycle motocross (BMX) events. John encouraged Jeff in these races.

Carol watched Jeff's BMX races. She thought the sport was too dangerous. She told Jeff that he could no longer race in BMX events.

Later that year, John bought Jeff and Kim a small racing machine called a quarter midget. These small racing cars look similar to go-karts. Drivers race quarter midgets on small dirt tracks. Quarter midgets have small motors that are about as powerful as lawn mower motors.

At first, Carol did not want Jeff to drive the quarter midget. But she saw that he was strapped into the machine and that he wore a helmet. She decided he was safer in his quarter midget than he was on a BMX bike. Carol began to encourage Jeff to practice racing quarter midgets.

Racing Quarter Midgets

Jeff liked his quarter midget. He practiced driving it in parking lots near his home. He

Jeff practiced racing for years to become a NASCAR driver.

wanted to enter quarter midget races. But he was too young. Quarter midget racing rules required drivers to be at least 5 years old. So Jeff kept practicing.

Jeff began entering quarter midget races as soon as he turned 5. He entered as many races as he could. He got better at driving the quarter midget with every race. He won 36 races in his second year of racing. When

he was 8, he won his first national quarter midget championship.

When Jeff was 9, he began racing go-karts. Go-karts have more powerful motors than quarter midgets do. They can travel at speeds as fast as 60 miles (97 kilometers) per hour. Jeff often raced against teenagers nearly twice his age. Most go-kart drivers were between the ages of 13 and 17. But Jeff kept winning his races. Few drivers wanted to race him by the time he was 10. The other drivers knew Jeff would beat them.

John saw that Jeff had great racing talent. John wanted to give Jeff new and difficult racing challenges. The two decided that Jeff would return to racing quarter midgets. They traveled across the United States to enter races and face new competition. Jeff raced almost every weekend. He also practiced two to three times per week.

Jeff's winning streak continued. He won every event he entered at age 10. He also

Jeff always looks for new racing challenges.

won a second national quarter midget championship. He soon became bored with quarter midgets.

Larger Cars

At age 13, Jeff developed an interest in sprint cars. Sprint cars are larger and more powerful than go-karts. But race organizers would not allow Jeff to take part in their races. They said he was too young. Rules required sprint car drivers to be at least 16 years old.

John and Jeff kept trying to find a way for Jeff to enter sprint car races. Finally, they convinced race officials to allow Jeff to race. Jeff did not win any of his early races. But he did prove that he was good enough to take part in the sport.

In 1986, Jeff's family moved to Pittsboro, Indiana. Race organizers in Indiana and the surrounding states allowed drivers younger than 16 to race sprint cars. There, Jeff could earn enough prize money to support his

Jeff knew at a young age that he wanted to be a professional driver.

family. John built and maintained an expensive sprint car for Jeff. John made sure all of the parts were in perfect working order. He sometimes made new parts to replace broken ones. Jeff and John traveled to races around the Midwest. The family lived off the money Jeff earned from these races. But they often did not have enough money to pay for hotel

rooms. Jeff and John sometimes had to sleep in their pickup truck when they traveled to races.

Jeff continued racing throughout high school. He slowly became famous among racing fans because of his talent and his age. The cable TV network ESPN even filmed a special feature about Jeff. The network showed the special on one of its racing shows.

Jeff decided that he wanted to become a professional driver after he graduated from high school. Jeff moved from racing sprint cars to midget cars. Midget cars are similar to quarter midgets. But they are larger and more powerful. In 1990, Jeff became the youngest driver ever to win the national midget car championship.

Jeff became famous for his talent at a young age.

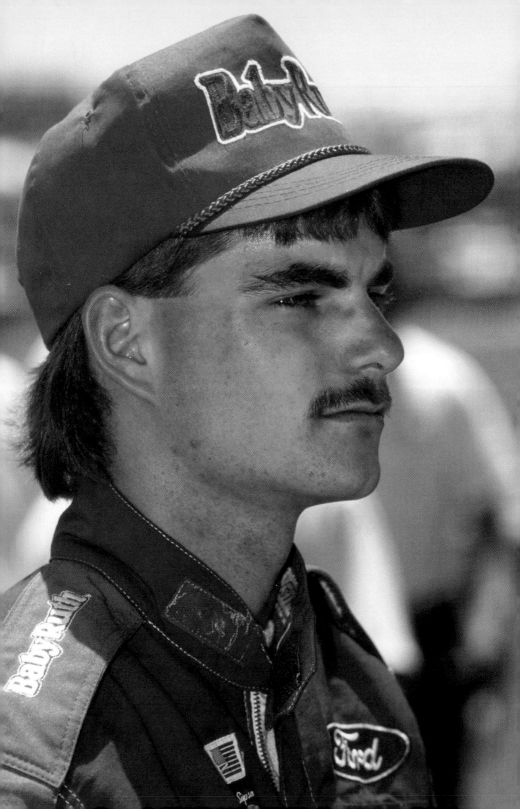

CHAPTER 3

Stock Car Racing

In 1990, Jeff and his parents decided Jeff should try racing stock cars. Drivers race these cars in NASCAR races. Stock cars have powerful engines. They can travel at speeds of more than 200 miles (320 kilometers) per hour.

Early Stock Car Racing

Jeff learned about a stock car racing school in Rockingham, North Carolina. A former racer named Buck Baker ran the school. Jeff attended Baker's school. It was his first chance to learn how to race stock cars. Jeff knew from his experience at Baker's school that he wanted

Jeff began his NASCAR career on the Busch Grand National Series.

to be a stock car driver. Jeff told John to sell all of their other cars and equipment.

Jeff soon proved that he was a skilled stock car driver. In 1991, he began racing in NASCAR's Busch Grand National Series. Later that year, he was named Rookie of the Year as the best first-year driver.

In 1992, Jeff raced again in the Busch Grand National Series. But he wanted to race in the Winston Cup series. The best stock car drivers in the world compete in this series. That year, a Winston Cup car owner named Rick Hendrick saw Jeff race. Hendrick asked Jeff to race for his team.

Winston Cup Racing

Jeff drove in his first Winston Cup race in 1992. It was the last race of the season at the Atlanta Motor Speedway in Atlanta, Georgia. No one paid much attention to Jeff during the race. He finished near the bottom of the race standings.

People noticed Jeff the next year. He started driving the number 24 car with the DuPont

Jeff drove the number 1 car in the Busch Grand National Series.

logo. Jeff's pit crew was called the Rainbow Warriors because of the colors of Jeff's car. With his team's help, Jeff proved that he was among the best young NASCAR drivers. Jeff did not win any Winston Cup races in 1993. But he did well in many of his races. In February 1993, Jeff became the youngest racer to win a qualifying race for the Daytona 500. This race takes place in Daytona, Florida. Jeff finished fifth in the race. This win was a great achievement for a young driver.

Jeff had his picture taken with model Brooke Sealy when he won the Daytona 500 qualifying race. Brooke had won a Miss Winston beauty contest that year. Jeff liked her right away. He asked her to go to lunch with him. Racing rules did not allow Brooke to date a driver. But Brooke and Jeff began to date in secret.

Many people had noticed Jeff's ability by the end of the 1993 season. He finished in 14th place among all Winston Cup drivers. He also was named Rookie of the Year for the Winston Cup series.

Jeff began racing in the Winston Cup series full-time in 1993.

CHAPTER 4

A New Star

Jeff had become one of the top young NASCAR drivers by the end of the 1993 season. Other drivers and racing fans saw that he had talent. Many believed that he could be one of the best drivers in the sport. During the 1994 season, Jeff proved them right.

First Victories

Jeff began the 1994 season by winning the Coca-Cola 600 at the Charlotte Motor Speedway in Charlotte, North Carolina. Jeff won by less than four seconds. After the race, Jeff sat in the winner's circle and cried. He was so happy to have won his first Winston

In 1994, Jeff won the first Brickyard 400.

Cup race. He called it the greatest moment of his life.

Jeff had another important victory in 1994. He won the first Brickyard 400 at the Indianapolis Motor Speedway in Indianapolis, Indiana. This race track was close to his home in Pittsboro. The race was close in the final laps. Jeff and drivers Ernie Irvan and Brett Bodine were leading the race. With five laps left, Irvan had tire problems. He fell behind. Jeff then took the lead. Jeff held that lead to beat Bodine by about four car lengths.

Jeff's popularity increased after those two wins. Fans wanted his autograph. They sometimes waited outside his trailer and followed him to the track. Jeff had become a star.

Jeff and Brooke married after the 1994 season. They moved into a house on the shore of Lake Norman in North Carolina. The lake is nicknamed Lake Speed because so many stock car drivers live there.

Jeff married Brooke Sealy in 1994.

A Championship Season

Jeff entered the 1995 season as a NASCAR star. But he wanted to finish the season as a Winston Cup champion.

Jeff and the Rainbow Warriors began the season well. They won three of the first six races. Jeff continued his success later in the season. He won the Pepsi 400 and the Mountain Dew Southern 500. Jeff kept winning later in the season. He gained a huge lead in the Winston Cup points standings. His lead was 300 points by the time he won the MBNA 500 in September. He easily won his first Winston Cup championship.

Jeff did make some mistakes during the 1995 season. In one race, Jeff made a pit stop for new tires. He thought his pit crew was going to change all four tires. He asked for a drink of water. But the crew changed only two tires. Jeff was not ready to go when the crew was done. He still was drinking. Jeff stalled his car when he realized that he had to go. These mistakes cost him valuable time. Jeff did not win the race. But he still came in second.

Jeff won his first Winston Cup championship in 1995.

Continued Success

Jeff had another successful year in 1996. He led the Winston Cup points standings for several months. He won 10 races that season. Some people thought he would win another title. But Terry Labonte won a series of races at the end of the season. Labonte won the championship. Jeff came in second.

Jeff returned in 1997 ready to win another championship. He began the season by winning the Daytona 500. At 25 years old, he was the youngest driver ever to win that race. He went on to win nine more races. When the season was over, Jeff had won his second Winston Cup championship. He beat second-place driver Dale Jarrett by only 14 points.

Jeff's greatest season may have been 1998. Jeff won the second race of the season. This race was the Goodwrench 400. By summer, Jeff was battling for the Winston Cup lead with two other drivers. These drivers were Jarrett and Mark Martin.

Jeff raced even better during the summer. He won four races in a row in July and August. These races were the Pennsylvania 500, the Brickyard 400, the Bud at the Glen, and the Pepsi 400. Only racing greats Richard Petty and Bobby Allison had won four races in a row. Jeff ended the season by winning the NAPA 500 in Atlanta, Georgia. This win was his 13th of the year. It helped him win his third Winston Cup championship.

Jeff began 1997 by winning the Daytona 500.

CHAPTER 5

Jeff Gordon Today

Jeff drives in about 33 Winston Cup races each year. He travels all over the United States. Winston Cup races are on Sundays. Jeff and Brooke fly to the racetracks in their private jet. They usually arrive on the Thursday before a race. Jeff sets up his gear in a trailer. He and Brooke live there until race day.

Jeff prepares for each race. He practices on the track before the race. He studies the track to find the best and worst places to pass other

---

Brooke travels around the country with Jeff to watch him race.

Ray Evernham quit as Jeff's crew chief in 1999.

cars. He also talks with his pit crew and crew chief to plan racing strategies.

The 1999 Season
The 1999 season was a difficult one for Jeff. He had problems with his car all year. He finished 1999 with seven DNFs (Did Not Finish) because of car trouble. Evernham also quit as crew chief.

Jeff began the season by winning his second Daytona 500. He had to hold off Dale Earnhardt in the closing laps to claim the victory. Jeff also won his first two races after Evernham left the team. In total, he won seven of the 34 races he started. No Winston Cup driver won more races in 1999. But several low race finishes and DNFs kept Jeff from winning his fourth Winston Cup championship. Jeff finished sixth in the points standings.

The 1999 season ended with an important announcement. Jeff and car owner Rick Hendrick entered into a lifetime agreement. The agreement means that Jeff now has a part ownership in his car and his team. It also means that Jeff will race the number 24 car for the rest of his career.

New Challenges

In 1999, Jeff formed his own Busch Grand National Series team. Jeff raced in six Busch Series events in 1999. He finished in the top five in four of these races. He won the Phoenix 500 in Phoenix, Arizona. In the future, Ricky

Hendrick may do most of the driving for the team. Ricky Hendrick is Rick Hendrick's son. Jeff may perform more management duties for the team. It will be a chance for him to prove that he can do more than drive.

Jeff also will have a greater involvement with his Winston Cup team in the future. Many of Jeff's crew members left the team in 1999. Jeff will have to find the right people to take their places.

Leukemia Society of America

Jeff serves as a volunteer for the Leukemia Society of America. His car's owner is fighting this form of blood cancer. Jeff also volunteers in honor of Evernham. Evernham's son also has leukemia.

The Leukemia Society of America is a group that helps doctors and scientists search for cures for leukemia and similar diseases. The society also works to improve the quality of life of patients and their families. Jeff makes public appearances and helps raise money for the Leukemia Society of America.

In the future, Jeff will perform more management duties for his teams.

Career Highlights

1971—Jeff is born on August 4 in Vallejo, California.

1976—Jeff begins racing quarter midgets.

1986—Jeff's family moves to Indiana so that Jeff can race sprint cars.

1991—Jeff begins racing stock cars in the Busch Grand National Series. He wins the Rookie of the Year award.

1992—Rick Hendrick discovers Jeff and signs him up to race for one of his NASCAR teams.

1993—Jeff wins NASCAR's Rookie of the Year award.

1994—Jeff wins his first Winston Cup race. He also wins the first Brickyard 400 at the Indianapolis Motor Speedway.

1995—Jeff wins his first Winston Cup championship.

1997—Jeff wins his second Winston Cup championship.

1998—Jeff wins 13 races and his third Winston Cup championship.

1999—Jeff signs a lifetime agreement with Rick Hendrick. He agrees to race for the number 24 team for the rest of his racing career.

Words to Know

crew chief (KROO CHEEF)—the member of a racing team who is in charge of maintaining the car; the crew chief also helps the driver choose racing strategies.

leukemia (loo-KEE-mee-uh)—a form of cancer that affects the blood

maintain (mayn-TAYN)—to keep a car in good racing condition

midget (MIJ-it)—a small racing vehicle; people drive midgets mainly on dirt tracks.

quarter midget (KWOR-tur MIJ-it)—a small racing vehicle built mainly for children; people drive quarter midgets mainly on dirt tracks.

rookie (RUK-ee)—a first-year driver

series (SIHR-eez)—a group of races that make up one season; drivers earn points for finishing races in a series.

To Learn More

Bach, Julie S. *Jeff Gordon.* Ovations. Mankato, Minn.: Creative Education, 1999.

Cain, Anthony B. *Jeff Gordon.* Sports Superstars. Chanhassen, Minn.: Child's World, 2000.

Center, Bill, and Bob Moore. *NASCAR 50 Greatest Drivers.* New York: HarperHorizon, 1998.

Kirkpatrick, Rob. *Jeff Gordon: NASCAR Champion.* Reading Power. New York: PowerKids Press, 2000.

Useful Addresses

Jeff Gordon (Autograph Requests and Fan Mail)
Personal Services Division
P.O. Box 515
Williams, AZ 86046-0515

Jeff Gordon Fan Club
1480 South Hohokam Drive
Tempe, AZ 85281

NASCAR Headquarters
1801 West International Speedway Boulevard
Daytona Beach, FL 32114

Internet Sites

Jeff Gordon Fan Club
http://www.speedmall.com/fanclubs/jeffgordon/
  fanclub

Jeff Gordon Online
http://www.gordonline.com

NASCAR Online
http://nascar.com

The Official Jeff Gordon Website
http://www.jeffgordon.com

Index